KU-256-256

About the Author

Andrew Ings has written many articles for a range of titles for over thirty years.

These have included theatrical reviews for a number of newspapers and magazines such as *Arts East*, *Centre Stage*, the *Jazz Rag*, *The Guardian* and *The London Evening Standard*.

Other articles have been sartorial regarding lifestyle and modern day life. In addition he has written pieces on cooking for men, health and exercise, cycling, country walking, health and safety and stress management. His first book was published in 2001.

Andrew was a contributor on a weekly radio programme on the arts for several years. He has been an advisor to a number of theatres in London, including Shakespeare's Globe and a major Academy of Theatrical Arts.

He is a board member for the Red Rose Chain Film and Theatre Company, and has also appeared in or directed many productions for local theatre groups.

He also appeared in the final episode of Blackadder.

His latest publication is a book on the history and birth place of British Rock 'n' Roll entitled *Rockin' at The 2i' Coffee Bar*.

A
NIPPERKIN
OF
BUNKUM

To Mike
with my best wishes

Many thanks to my wife Muriel for help with proofreading for these scripts, and also some ideas which have been incorporated. Also thanks to my son Alex who had the idea for a stag night for an 85 year old.

Andrew Ings

A
NIPPERKIN
OF
BUNKUM

Non-PC comedy sketches
(Long live free speech)

AUSTIN & MACAULEY
PUBLISHERS LTD.

Copyright © Andrew Ings

The right of Andrew Ings to be identified as author of this work has been asserted by him in accordance with section 77 and 78 of the Copyright, Designs and Patents Act 1988.

All rights reserved. No part of this publication may be reproduced, stored in a retrieval system, or transmitted in any form or by any means, electronic, mechanical, photocopying, recording, or otherwise, without the prior permission of the publishers.

Any person who commits any unauthorized act in relation to this publication may be liable to criminal prosecution and civil claims for damages.

A CIP catalogue record for this title is available from the British Library.

ISBN 9781849633208

www.austinmacauley.com

First Published (2013)
Austin & Macauley Publishers Ltd.
25 Canada Square
Canary Wharf
London
E14 5LB

Printed & Bound in Great Britain

AUTHOR'S NOTE

All of the pieces in this collection are designed to be staged with minimal props, etc.

These sketches work because they are pictures of life as seen by most or all of us at different times.

They comment on things that we have become too shy to shout about because of the nonsense of political correctness and all the hypocritical rubbish that it has created.

Some items contain elements of conversations or incidents which I have personally experienced.

CONTENTS

CHATTER BOXES..15

INTRODUCTION 17

THE TURNER PRIZE? 18

SYMPHONY FOR ONE.............................25

NEWS ITEMS 29

THE HAGGIS 32

THE INTERVIEW 36

EXCHANGE ENQUIRIES..........................41

DRESS CODE...46

THINKING ALOUD 51

A FEW WORDS...58

AM I ENGLISH – OR WHAT? 61

SEW 68

GRAB IT AND RUN...................................73

SHOPPING...77

OPENING AN ACCOUNT 80

PARTY POLITICAL BROADCAST..............84

WHAT STAG NIGHT? 87

CHATTER BOXES

Use this to introduce the cast, so 'talk script' as they walk from rear of hall.

[Scene: A party or cocktail 'do'. Various people holding drinks and chatting.
Dialogue could be between males or females or mixed – depending on casting ease.
Style: smart/trendy.]

A: [Approaching B]
       And you are?
B: Yes – are you?
A: Sorry?
B: What for?
A: What do you mean 'what for'?
B: You said you were sorry.
A: Did I?
B: Yes.
C: That's what I like to hear.
A: Pardon?
B: Granted.
A: What?
C: Someone being positive.
B: What do you mean?
C: 'Yes' – that's positive – you said 'yes'.
B: Did I?
A: Yes you did.
B: Why, what have you done?
A: Oh God, here we go again.
D: What, are you going already?
C: What?

D:	He said you were going.
C:	Did he?
A:	No, I did not.
B:	Didn't what?
C:	Say you were going.
D:	Sorry, I erm … misheard.
E:	What?
D:	Miss Heard.
C:	Who is Miss Heard?
D:	No one.
A:	Why talk about no one?
D:	We're not talking about 'no one'.
E:	So you are talking about someone?
D:	No.
E:	Why not?
D:	Look, it's perfectly simple.
B:	Nothing is ever that simple.
C:	'Nothing' is always simple, because it's nothing.
A:	Well, I'm glad that's over.
D:	So you are going?
C:	No – he is [points to 'A'].

VO: **'Ladies and gentlemen, you can come through now'.**

[They start to move offstage]

A:	Look, for the last time, I am not going.
B:	What about Miss Heard?
E:	I think she has gone.
C:	Has she? What, before we go in?
E:	She'd had enough, I think.
D:	I say, this is a great party – such interesting conversation.

[BLACK OUT]

INTRODUCTION

MC:
Good evening everyone and welcome to an evening of non-politically correct fun.

Before we begin the show, will you please ensure that all electrical items are switched off. This includes phones, alarm clocks which you brought in case you fall asleep, pace makers and other – erm – vibrating devices.

Various announcements will be made during the evening so please listen carefully in case they are relevant to you.

Please be aware that opinions expressed in the announcements may not reflect the views of management – except that they are paying to advertise – so that's good, innit? Oh, here is the first one.

VO:
May I remind all in the audience that there is strictly no smoking allowed in any part of the building. However, if you are smoking a joint, it's only fair that you share it with those sitting near you.

So, without further ado, we now go live to the Banal studios to join Jo King's chat show.

THE TURNER PRIZE?

[Scene – Commercial TV chat show.]

Characters;- Joe King, Interviewer – A stand-in for the usual guy. Very down to earth character – calls a spade a spade. Totally wrong for a high brow slot. Not given to abstract or totally surrealistic art form. In every sense out of his depth and sounds 'common'. Easily blinded by science or 'bullshit baffles brains'. Makes the error of calling Hughe 'HUGE'.

Hughe Perciman-Smythe – Fine art critic and surrealist specialist. Speaks with an extreme plum in the mouth (extra posh accent). Supposed guru of 21st century abstract art and doyen of third age creations.

Director's Notes:
Joe is very common and sounds it – drops word endings, etc. Hughe speaks rather slowly and deliberately, EM – PHA – SIS – ING every syllable.

[As house lights go down, *VO* speaks]

"Okay, ladies and gentlemen, we are only a minute away from going on air. When the curtains open and the lights come up, please give a warm welcome to tonight's presenter JOE KING"

Joe: Watcha mates. Sorry that Parky can't be here tonight, so I'm a brilliant stand-in in for him. I'm only joking. No, really, I'm Joe King. The first thing we are going to talk about is the latest showing of the Third Age Movement at the Cutpurse Gallery, which I was forced to go and see last week. To discuss it I am joined in the studio by... er... [drops notes on floor – gathers them up while moaning] oh hell, sorry, er... half a mo, ah yes – Huge Perciman-Smythe, art critic of the *Preposterous Quarterly* and doyen of the 3rd age movement. At least that's what it says here.

[Enter Hughe]

Greetings Huge, nice to see you.

Hughe:	Hughe.
Joe:	Pardon?
Hughe:	Hughe – my name is Hughe, darling, not 'huge'.
Joe:	Oh, so sorry mate.
Hughe:	Well, normally I would be delighted to be here, but really, the colour co-ordination in this new studio – well, my dear, it does leave one... well, disorientated, don't you know.
Joe:	Yes, well, no doubt them makeover people did their rehearsal in here. But anyway, tell us about this latest controversial exhibition at the Cutpurse Gallery which I've been told contains a contender for the Turner Prize.
Hughe:	Well, you call it controversial. But I, of course, do not agree. But whether it is or not is in the intellect of the sapian who has the wit to consider it.
Joe:	Sorry – sapian? What are you on about?
Hughe:	My dear man [patronising] Sapiens – Homo sapiens – you and me.
Joe:	Here just a minute who are you calling a homo?
Hughe:	Homo! Homo sapiens – mankind – all of us.
Joe:	So, not queer then?
Hughe:	[Very camp] Queer – my dear? Certainly not.
Joe:	You're sure about that, are you?
Hughe:	[Very camp] I am sure YOU are not queer.
Joe:	Right, that's a relief. So, what is the chief attraction in the show?

Hughe:	Well, reluctant as one is to admit such a thing, one has to admit that, albeit reluctantly the star exhibit is by an artist called Emanual Myopica. An artist from Los Angeles – I believe plebs refer to the place as LA – who has put in something simple yet infinitely imaginative.
Joe:	Really? So what's it called, this star exhibit?
Hughe:	The Great American Doughnut.
Joe:	The Great American Doughnut?
Hughe:	Yes. Exactly so.
Joe:	But when I went to see it there was nothing there.
Hughe:	What do you mean, 'nothing there'?
Joe:	As I said mate, the area in the gallery was – like – empty – nothing there.
Hughe:	Ah, my dear man, but you see, that is because it had become embodied within Emanual Myopica's persona, allowing him to become part of the exhibit.
Joe:	What do you mean?
Hughe:	Well, in common layman terms, he consumed it. Thus experiencing [Waves arms about extravagantly] the interaction between the artist and the creation.
Joe:	What do you mean he consumed it?
Hughe:	Well, he ate it.
Joe:	He et it?
Hughe:	Yes, exactly so. He experienced the ultimate in artistic creation.
Joe:	But he scoffed the bun.
Hughe:	No, my dear man – he became at one with the manifestation of his creative thought.
Joe:	What? What on earth are you on about?
Hughe:	Well, he was totally in unison with his artistic self.
Joe:	What's that supposed to mean?
Hughe:	He was his creation.
Joe:	But the fact is, there is nothing there to see.
Hughe:	Ah, but there is, you see, my good fellow.
Joe:	Okay, so what?

Hughe:	Well, the doughnut was a ring – a symbol of all of life's cycle – whilst at the same time, that creation of culinary lightness that has a space in the middle, and so when he consumes the edible section of his creation he – as it were – becomes at one with his creation.
Joe:	You mean when he et it?
Hughe:	Well, if you insist.
Joe:	Well that's what he did, didn't he?
Hughe:	The point is, he was at one with the centre edge of the space and in removing this barrier it allows us all to experience the inner space. You see, he took a holistic approach, thus eating the whole doughnut, so allowing the hole to expand to infinity.
Joe:	Sorry Huge – let's get this straight – the exhibit...
Hughe:	Hughe, Hughe.
Joe:	– was a doughnut with a hole in the middle.
Hughe:	Well, if you put in such basic terms – yes.
Joe:	And he et the doughnut, so in fact there is nothing there to see – no exhibit!
Hughe:	Ah, but you see, one has the sublime realisation of space being created, whilst at the same time the artist recreates the shape of the doughnut.
Joe:	How?
Hughe:	By the rhythmic coordination and juxtaposition of the lower and upper facial frame, don't you know.
Joe:	Pardon me, but what are you talking about?
Hughe:	He masticates –
Joe:	Here, just a minute – this a family show.
Hughe:	– He masticates – chews very slowly, savouring every exquisite and tiny morsel – and in doing so, simultaneously becomes at one with his creation whilst at the same time is instrumental in creating another exhibit.
Joe:	Another exhibit?
Hughe:	Yes. The space which was surrounded by the first exhibit now becomes ours to enjoy. It is an

	imaginary journey in which the artist encourages us to expand our thoughts and feelings for this new space – if you like, becoming enveloped in the holistic experience of being in the whole hole.
Joe:	So by getting rid of something we can create a space for others to experience?
Hughe:	Yes, exactly that. You see, experience is everything to our inner selves or, to put it another way, the cosmic space within us. Remember, we are talking about the cosmic relationship between space and emptiness.
Joe:	Sorry, I thought we were talking about the geezer who et a doughnut.
Hughe:	Yes, exactly that. He consumed the physical to create the cosmic for us all to enjoy.
Joe:	So, would you say that Emanual Myopica was artistically effluential?
Hughe:	Sorry, don't you mean influential?
Joe:	Well, as I understand it, influential is persuasion by wisdom.
Hughe:	But you said 'effluential'.
Joe:	Yes, that's someone who tries to influence others by coming out with a load of crap about nothing.
Hughe:	I say, just a minute. There is no need to be rude.
Joe:	You have been going on about homos in cosmic something or other and a bun that does not exists. To me that's a load of crap.
Hughe:	Now, hold on …
Joe:	[Interrupting] Before we take a break, I can announce that alongside the Turner Prize the following are the hot favourites in the lineup for Thinnest Book Title awards.

"The Power of Thinking" by George W. Bush,
"The Benefits of Celibacy" by Silvio Berlusconi,
"My Joy and Love of Live Theatre" by the Indian critic
Pandit Fiercely,
"How to Run an Honest Business" by Rupert Murdoch.

[Turns to the audience]

Now it's time to take a break. We will be back later with my next guest.

[BLACK OUT]

VO:	**HERE IS A HEALTH AND SAFETY ANNNOUNCMENT.**

"Please be advised that when the fire alarm sounds, it may mean that something is on fire"

SYMPHONY FOR ONE

A MONOLOGUE WITH A LITTLE HELP

DIRECTORS NOTE:
It is essential that this be read 'straight' and in a strict Radio 3 voice. Any attempt to emphasise the humour would destroy it.
The announcer would be in a tuxedo and ideally at a stand mic.
Thin could wear anything eccentric. If possible, get someone with a 'rubber face' to play Thin, with facial expressions developing as his frustration grows.

Announcer: [Down stage either Right or Left – in a slightly hushed voice]

> And now we are joined by listeners to Radio 3, whom I would like to welcome to today's lunchtime concert, coming to you live from the Wigmore Hall here in the heart of London. The programme for today's recital is based on a suite of works originally composed by Klaus Trophobe.
> The indifferent of you may like to recall that he is the only known composer of works for the pianoforte who, as well as being totally deaf, was unable to play a single note. However, it is very much to his credit that after concentrated study for nearly thirty years he did manage to master that singular and most minimalist of all instruments. Indeed, he was to become a world

authority on the instrument and towards the end of his life was made a Fellow of the Society of Metallurgists for his work in developing the triangle.

We are very privileged today to welcome a soloist of considerable talent. He is a man who has variously been described.
The first piece that Ebeenezer Thin is going to play is entitled Ab Maseto Neno.
Those in the audience still awake will immediately recognise it as a modern interpretation of the popular One Note Samba. However, here it is played backwards.
Ebeneezer re-worked this adaptation during a particularly unhappy period in his life, considerable stress being caused, in fact, by a triangle. His wife ran away with his music teacher.
This was a double blow, as apart from being without a teacher, he was also without his musical partner with whom he did many live street performances.
This form of entertaining was very popular among those residents of the Waterloo precinct and appealed to their minimalist style of life. They could oft be heard on the steps of Waterloo Bridge or under one of the arches, playing with each other.
If we listen carefully, especially to the middle section, we can hear the anguish of this period vividly portrayed. Although the work is performed here on the pianoforte, the strong influence of the simple – one could even say utterly boring in the constructive nuance – monotone of the strident clang of the hammer on the triangle does manage to get through.

It is interesting to note that when this was first performed in Vienna, the whole house rose to its feet in universal rupture. I am so sorry, that should read universal rapture.

You will, I am sure, note that this simplistic approach is the main hallmark of his work. Indeed, so astounded were his contemporaries, particularly what one might call the establishment, that on one notable occasion the audience greeted his solo performance of a single note with tumultuous indifference.

Ecstatic he became Brahms and List – I am sorry, that should read 'ecstatic he came to Brahms and List to discover further techniques in the development of playing single notes'.

And now, will you please welcome Ebeneezer Thin.

ENTER THIN;- [Opposite side from Announcer. His hand is heavily bandaged, save for one finger. He walks very slowly and ceremoniously down centre and bows. He then has trouble in standing up as his back is 'gone' . He is very large.]

ANNOUNCER: Just before we commence this performance, I would like to give you some biographical details of our distinguished soloist.

[Thin continues across the stage to take his seat at the piano – a key board could double – and meticulously arranges himself at the keyboard]

He was born in 1937, the only son of a bitch – I am sorry, the only son of a bitumen salesman.

[Thin again prepares to play]

The musical influence in his early life was undoubtedly his father, whom, as well as being a bell-ringer in the local prison church, was a drummer in an Irish string quartet.

Young Ebeneezer's first actual experience of music was to occur in the bell tower of the local church. After he attended several practice sessions of bell-ringing, he apparently committed some minor misdemeanour and was as a result tied to one of the bell ropes and tolled off. The bell was set in motion for a peal that was to last for more than five hours. Thus was created a record for the longest single peal by a junior campanoligist.

[Thin again prepares to play.]

After this event, his musical direction took an unexpected turn and he was soon deep in the study of the bass drum, subsequently taking his father's place in the string quartet.

Sadly another mishap altered his life, for whilst rehearsing for a drum roll, he lost control of the instrument, careering down a hill to collide with a vehicle which belonged to the local constabulary, injuring his hands in the process.

By this time, the idea of the single note performance was firmly established in his mind and he took up serious historical study and research in the hallowed halls of the library in Wormwood Scrubs.

The results of that study we are today privileged to witness.

[Thin braces himself, is positively poised to strike the note.]

Ladies and Gentlemen, I am most terribly sorry – we appear to have run out of time and I must now hand you back to the studio for the latest news.

[Thin raises a single finger in defiance.]

[BLACK OUT]

NEWS ITEMS

[News cast music intro 10 or 20 seconds]

[Scene: News desk similar to the Two Ronnies.
Piles of paper in front of each of 2 readers.]

A: Good afternoon. Here is the news. I am Peregrine Farquarh-Smyth.

B: And I am Wanda Handful.

A: Commenting on a complaint from a Mr. Arthur Purdey about a large gas bill, a spokesman for North West Gas said, 'We agree it was rather high for the time of year. It's possible Mr. Purdey has been charged for the gas used during the explosion that destroyed his house.

B: Police reveal that a woman arrested for shoplifting had a whole salami in her underwear. When asked why, she said it was because she was missing her Italian boyfriend.

A: Local police are being handicapped in a search for a stolen van, because they cannot issue a description. It's a Special Branch vehicle and they don't want the public to know what it looks like.

B: A young girl who was blown out to sea on a set of inflatable teeth was rescued by a man on an inflatable lobster. A coast guard spokesman commented, 'This sort of thing is all too common'.

At the height of the gale, the harbour master radioed a coast guard and asked him to estimate the wind speed. He replied he was sorry, but he didn't have a gauge. However, if it was any help, the wind had just blown his Land Rover off the cliff.

A: Mrs. Irene Graham of Thorpe Avenue, Boscombe, delighted the audience with her reminiscence of the German prisoner of war who was sent each week to do her garden. He was repatriated at the end of 1945, she recalled - 'He'd always seemed a nice friendly chap, but when the crocuses came up in the middle of our lawn in February 1946, they spelt out 'Heil Hitler."

B: A new Health and Safety booklet has been issued by the Dutch Government.

It requires special fire precautions to be in place in brothels which specialise in sado-masochism practices in case clients are too tied up to be able to make a quick escape.

Dutch town council officials will be inspecting and testing the establishments to ensure they are toeing the line.

A: And now for some other stories. It was reported that a women in Glasgow wrote the following letter to Social Services.

"I am glad to state that my husband died. I will be glad if you will get the pension for me. If you don't hurry up with it, I will have to get Public Resistance."

B: Yes, and here is another one.

       "Please send me a form for cheap milk. I have a baby two months old and did not know anything about it until a neighbour told me".

A: And finally,
       "In accordance with your instructions I have given birth to twins in the enclosed envelope".

B: And with that, it is good night to you all from Wanda and Peregrine.

       [Repeat news music]

         [BLACKOUT]

THE HAGGIS

Directors Note: This is a lecture – a wind up so the style is flexible. The actor could be at a lectern.

Speaker: Good evening. First, let me say how nice it is to be back at the National Centre of Conservation Studies.

Today we are going to the far North of Scotland and I am going to talk to you about a vanishing Scottish species.

Back through the mists and mysteries of Scottish history, there were creatures that inhabited mountain tops each side of Loch Nether.

To the north was the Haarg and on the south side lived the Essy. The Haarg and the Essy continuously fought over territory in the Nether regions in their attempt to survive.

Haarg would cast a spell, leaving Essy with long red ears. Essy would respond by turning Haarg's suit of armour into a tartan skirt, implying he was really female.

Haarg followed this by turning the face of Essy into a vole-like creature with a pointed nose and crossed eyes. A more recent manifestation had the name of Mr Bean.

Their shrieks and moans continued with ever increasing imagination as they cast their spells on each other.

Now the Celts heard this and became frightened, and so it was many years before they ventured in to the Nether regions.

Finally when they did, they discovered strange fur-covered creatures in the hills. Remembering the fearsome cry, they named them Haargess.

The Haargess or haggis as it became known is, in fact, quite unique in the animal kingdom, having a very pronounced limp. This is especially evident when the little fellow is perambulating on level ground.

You see, in that environment his disability did create stability problems, the fact being that his front and rear legs on the left hand side are twice as long as those on the opposite side.

This imbalance has developed over many generations as a result of a desire to run clockwise around the top of the hills and mountains.

The habit developed as a result of its favourite diet – the mosquito – always flying anticlockwise around the hills. Thus, by running with its mouth wide open, his meal was assured as the mosquito flew straight into the oncoming mouth. Interestingly, their cousins Down Under do the exact opposite.

Nature, always responding to the need for survival, thus encouraged the extra leg growth on the port or left side.

Think about it for a few moments. If you walk or run around a peak where the ground is closer to one foot than the other, you will fall over. But not the Haggis.

So, we must now seek to protect the species having re-established itself.

Today we are launching a preservation order to stop the hunting by the kilt brigade.

But in the far north of Scotland where women are women and the men wear skirts, how do you tell the difference?

Each has a patch of fur in their lap, the difference being that the skirt-wearing male has it on the outside. And what is that, you ask?

It is the pelt of a haggis, for you are not considered a true man in the north unless you wear a skirt decorated with the pelt of a haggis dangling down the front. It is what we now call a sporran.

As a result, the haggis is now becoming rare due to over-hunting in the mistaken belief that the meat of the haggis has some aphrodisiac powers.

So, next time you are in Scotland or see a haggis on the menu do resist the temptation to eat it. Have a nessy steak instead. A nessy steak, you ask?

Well that's the subject of my next talk here at the National Centre of Conservation Studies. Goodnight, and I thank you from the heart of my bottom.

[BLACK OUT]

VO: And now for a cookery lesson.

        Remember, you can make a wonderful nourishing broth
        from the remains if you have an invalid in the house.

THE INTERVIEW

[Scene: An office – desk chair etc.]

CHARACTERS:

HE -   Thirty-ish – a 'suit'.
SHE -   Essex girl type, seventeen-ish, dumb.
         She must be good at ad-libbing monosyllabic rubbish for
         about 20 seconds every time her phone rings.
         "Hi ya – you all right – yea right – no really", etc, etc.

HE: Come in Miss, er, [Looks at paper] Chatterton.
             [Points to chair]
SHE: Ta, thanks. [She sits]
HE: Now, I see from your application that you
             appear not to have much experience.
SHE: Well, I've done a couple of months and... [Her
             mobile rings. She chats, 'says nothing']
             Sorry about that.
HE: That's okay. Now, tell me a little about yourself.
SHE: Well, I ain't married. Got several boyfriends
             though – like to play the field – know what I
             mean? – and love to party.
HE: Well, about qualifications – I see that...
SHE: [Interrupting]
             Well, I did a business course at the local
             college.
HE: Oh, very good. Two years, was it?
SHE: No, just the weekend. Should be enough,
             shouldn't it?
HE: Well, I was rather hoping that...

SHE:	[Interrupting] Then I did a computer course – you know the foundation – on Monday morning. But apart – [Her phone rings again] 'Scuse me. [More stupid chatter] [Hangs up] Sorry 'bout that.
HE:	You were saying?
SHE:	Was I? Oh yes, well, I've done a couple of introductory courses so I feel really cool about doing your job.
HE:	My job?
SHE:	Well, not your job but you know, the job I'm 'ere for.
HE:	Do you know anything about communication skills?
SHE:	Commuy what kills?
HE:	[Spells it out] Communication skills.
SHE:	What do you mean?
HE:	Communication. Relating to other people.
SHE:	Oh that, yeah. I've got lots of relatives.
HE:	No, I mean relating to other people.
SHE:	Sorry?
HE:	Talking.
SHE:	Oh, talking.
HE:	Exactly that. Yes, in fact, *listening* to what other people have to say, especially when you are on the phone.
SHE:	Oh no, I couldn't do that. [Her phone rings again. She chats] Sorry 'bout that.
HE:	You couldn't?
SHE:	No way.
HE:	Why not?
SHE:	Well, people go on about stuff don't they? Stuff I can't be bothered with.
HE:	Well, why are you here?
SHE:	Well, I want the job I applied for. [Phone rings. Chats] Sorry 'bout that.
HE:	And what is that, exactly?
SHE:	What is what exactly?

HE:	You were saying – before you were interrupted – AGAIN...
SHE:	Sorry, I ought to have switched it off, shouldn't I? But the bloke in the shop told me I get points for every call I get, so I get me mates to ring me all the time. Sorry, what did you ask me?
HE:	Do you know how to?
SHE:	How to what?
HE:	Switch it off.
SHE:	Yes, you press – oh, you're having a laugh, aren't you?
HE:	Not exactly.
SHE:	What do you mean?
HE:	You seem inseparable from your phone.
SHE:	Well, it's all me mates – they call me all the time – or text me. Like I said I get points –
HE:	Are all the calls necessary?
SHE:	What do you mean?
HE:	Well, you've had several calls since you came in.
SHE:	Yeah, sorry 'bout that, it was Shirl.
HE:	Shirl?
SHE:	Yes, she wants to know how I got on with the job interview and if I passed my exam.
HE:	And how do you think you have got on?
SHE:	Well, I'm not sure, really. You haven't really asked me a lot, and anyway, it's my very first ever interview, actually.
HE:	Really, your first interview? But exam, what exam?
SHE:	Well, I've just finished a course on... [Her phone rings] Hello, yes – oh wow – great ta, ever so. [Hangs up] Oh. So sorry – what was I saying?
HE:	About your exam.
SHE:	[Her voice now Sloane] Oh yes rather – well actually it was a course in elocution, actually.
HE:	[Taken aback]

– Well, well, well. Erm, in actual fact... [His phone rings]

Yes, yes, yes. She's fine. Very chatty, but doesn't listen and hasn't got a grain of intelligence. She will be ideal. [Hangs up]

Sorry, so when can you start?

SHE: Start? You mean, I've got the job?

HE: Yes, I think you will fit in very well. We need people like you to work in our new customer service call centre.

[BLACK OUT]

VO: Here is an announcement regarding audience enjoyment.

"If your mobile phone rings during the performance it may be surgically removed by our stage technician."

"Also, please be aware that in the next sketch alcohol may be consumed. Well, some people get all the luck."

EXCHANGE ENQUIRIES

A piece about the very irritating phenomena of call centres and the demise of a very efficient 192 system.

[Scene: This could be done as a monologue with VO or an actress could be on one side of a split set at a desk with a computer and a headset with the caller opposite at a desk or in an easy chair 'at home'.

She should remain very calm – her speech should sound as if it is a recorded message – in her response as a total contrast to him slowly going round the bend with frustration.]

As the curtain opens, she is looking bored and doing her nails.
He is looking through the Yellow Pages, then puts them down having not found the number.

Him:	[Looking at paperwork, dials a number]
	[PHONE RINGS]
Her:	[Reading from a prepared text]
	Thank you for calling the Aquarius Personal Directory Enquiries Service.
Him:	Oh God, not another robot. [Looks at watch]
Her:	Be assured of personal service from Aquarius at all times.
Him:	[Mutters and curses]
Her:	You will now be offered a choice from Aquarius Personal Directory Enquiry Services –
Him:	Just get on with it. [Looks at watch
Her:	Personal service is our motto.
Him:	So prove it. [Pen at ready]

Her:	Please speak slowly, spelling any unusual words like London, York or Devon and state the name for which you would like the number.
Him:	Greystone Construction, Colchester. [Resigned sigh]
Her:	Is that Greystone Destruction, Cirencenster?
Him:	[Disbelief] No, Greystone Construction, Colchester.
Her:	Aquarius Personal Directory Enquiry Services are susceptible to mood changes that manifest themselves through changes in your voice. Please remain calm and repeat your enquiry
Him:	[Begins to moan. Takes breath. Louder] Greystone Construction, Colchester.
Her:	We at Aquarius Personal Directory Enquiry Services pride ourselves in being accurate. Is that Greystone Destruction?
Him:	[Almost as an aside] Hoo bloody ray, after a minute one word out of three is right. Yes, yes, Greystone CONSTRUCTION, Colchester.
Her:	If we are correct and have impressed you with our prized personal service, please press 1 now. If we have part of your enquiry correct, please press 2 now. If you have a query, please press 3 now. For all other enquiries, please press 4 now.
Him:	Oh, for God's sake. [presses 2]
Her:	Thank you. Please keep calm. We at Aquarius Personal Directory Enquiries Services are susceptible to emotional frustration that leads to manifestation in voice changes.
Him:	Pity you aren't sensitive to what people want. Right, I'll press 2 now. [Really shouts. Reaches for whiskey bottle and takes a swig]
Her:	Aquarius Personal Directory Enquiries Service note your agreement for Greystone. Please repeat clearly the remaining part of the enquiry.
Him:	[Takes another swig] Yes, yes, Greystone CONSTRUCTION in Colchester.
Her:	Is that Construction? If we are correct and have achieved our prized personal service, please

	press 1 now. If we have part of your enquiry correct, please press 2 now. If you have a query, please press 3 now. For all other enquiries, please press 4 now.
Him:	[Presses 2 and curses. Laughs] Yes, yes, yes.
Her:	Thank you. One moment please while we at Aquarius Personal Directory Enquiries Service analyse your request. [He takes another swig] We have 9 listings for Greystone Construction.
Him:	Thank God for that. At last, I am getting somewhere.
Her:	Please state your desired location so that we at Aquarius Personal Directory Enquiries Service can be of assistance.
Him:	[Spells is out] C O L C H E S T E R.
Her:	Is that Colchester? If we are correct and have achieved our prized personal service, please press 1 now. If we have part of your enquiry correct, please press 2 now. If you have a query, please press 3 now. For all other enquiries, please press 4 now.
Him:	Yes, yes, yes. [Beginning to become hysterical. Takes another swig and bangs phone with fist]
Her:	Please state which area that is in.
Him:	[In disbelief, shouts] It is in Essex!
Her:	So that we at Aquarius Personal Directory Enquiries can be of assistance, please state in which county Essex is in.
Him:	What!? [Takes a big swig, opens another bottle, continues. Explodes, then sobs] Essex is the county, you bloody moron.
Her:	We at Aquarius Personal Directory Enquiries Service are susceptible to mood swings even on the telephone. Please control yourself. The number which you are seeking does not exist.
Him:	What!? It's been there for thirty bloody years! [Sobs, slams phone down. Drinks another swig. Sobbing with frustration, picks up Yellow Pages again. Finds number and dials]
Him	Hello, is that the Samaritans?

[BLACK OUT]

VO: "Please be aware that in this next item there is some flash photography. Oh no, sorry – just flashing."

DRESS CODE

A monologue

[Scene: The board meeting.
The MD sits so he cannot be seen from the waist down to address the meeting (the audience).
He is in a suit and tie from the waist up. When he finishes his speech, he leans down to pick up a handbag. When he stands we see that he is in a skirt and tights with high heels.
During the monologue various names are mentioned. These can be changed to fit your crew or colleagues.]

[TABS OPEN]

MD: Members of the Board, as you know, for some time now we have been considered trendsetters amongst our competitors in this area.

Remember, it was our company in my predecessor's day who first declared the bowler hat and umbrella , those symbols of a bye-gone age, as completely redundant.

Later there came the coloured shirt. No longer was it necessary to wear white.

As time went by, we were the first to adopt the fashion that Friday became 'dress down day'. This was followed by a relaxation throughout the week corresponding, I may say, with increased performance from all our colleagues.

However, there were some interesting moments when fancy dress began to appear.

I did begin to wonder at the wisdom of this when Steve from accounts welcomed our visitor from Japan dressed as a samurai. I understand that he belongs to a martial arts club but I do feel that appearing to threaten our biggest Far Eastern customer with a samurai sword was going a bit too far.

Indeed, the sword was extremely sharp and nearly resulted in a sex change operation for our visitor.

You know, our male colleagues really must be more careful with their weapons.

Then there was Barbara from IT. Normally, if I may say so, she is the very model of a modern lady feminine. A real 'IT' girl. Barbara, as some of you may know, often spends her lunch hour dressed in male attire – as a Bishop actually – pole dancing in the Red Lion which as you all know is – rather unfortunately – next door to the parish church.

Regrettably, following the visit here by members of the synod to discuss gay rights within the church, we had taken them to the Red Lion for lunch. Some were quite naturally a little shocked when Barbara called a welcome to me whilst [Hesitates] ' manoeuvering' herself around the pole and even jokingly accused me of taking in some competition.

However, the mood lightened when two of the clergy actually began to join in and others asked for an encore.

That reminds me – I must remember to ask Barbara if she has ever been 'anointed' by any of them.

I would like to mention a couple more of our colleagues before I get to the main proposals.

Dear Patrick in Sales, bless his silk pyjamas.

[Pauses when he realises what he has said]

He is such a wag – just loves dressing up. I saw him in Dorothy Perkins only last weekend and I told him, I said that little skirt really suits you. He was so surprised to see me coming out of the fitting room opposite his. [Pauses] As he said, "at least you're not getting the same colour as me!" [Laughs]

I must just mention Marion – she is the star of the HR dept. [As an aside] That's Human Resources, although when you look at her, you could be forgiven for thinking it meant Hormone Replacement. With her ability to grow facial hair, she is sometimes admirably dressed up as a gamekeeper accompanied by dear Chris with her dark and rustic complexion perfectly dressed as Mellors. They can often be seen in the Butch Cassidy club strutting their fluff.

Patrick and Steve we have already mentioned, so now let's turn to Tim, also in IT.

They don't come much butcher than Tim. Interesting that he likes to dress in white aprons – sometimes not much else.

I first met the old rogue in the 'Engine Room', a really powerful and throbbing wine bar. [Smiles] I just happened to pop in there one evening – quite by chance, you understand. And there in the middle of a fine collection of muscles was this gorgeous head of blonde hair. As his head turned, I realised who it was. I never knew Tim had such a beautiful blond wig.

Now, a few words about our sales force who regularly come face to face with our customers, sometimes resulting in high blood pressure due to the customers' misplaced anger and frustration. The more observant of you will have noticed that the team has begun to wear designer miniskirts. The ladies, of course, look natural, but the gentlemen have had to get used to shaving their legs.

Anyway, the idea is that a feminine appearance defuses some situations. So, with that in mind, and so many of our colleagues well placed to set the new trend here is my idea.

[Takes drink from glass]

Building on our Friday dress down day, I propose that from the beginning of next month to have – throughout the office – a cross dressing day. [Pause]

Now, before you all complain about the delay, we really do have to wait until next month, bearing in mind that some of our colleagues will need to do some shopping to bring their wardrobe up to speed.

I need hardly remind you that the city will be watching us closely. Our recruitment department are expecting an influx of applications from some members of parliament, especially those who may not keep their seats at the next election.

We will, of course, be arranging visits by costumiers to advise on appropriate items of clothing and style to assist you with your day as a transvestite. In addition, we will be recruiting the services of a certain politician to advise on mannerisms of being a bisexual.

Well, if there are no questions I must bring this meeting to a close as I have an appointment with my beautician.

Thank you for listening.

[Picks up handbag and stands to reveal skirt, tights and high heels]

[BLACK OUT]

VO*:*   This is from the 1st Book of Perversions – verse sex

        "And the Harlot sayeth unto the man of the sea, 'hello sailor' and did lead him in kinky ways"

THINKING ALOUD

(Out of the mouths of babes and sucklings)

DIRECTORS NOTE;
This sketch will need a pre-recorded 'voice over' or someone in the wings on a mic. The timing of the VO will have to be tight if maximum humour is to be achieved. The younger the voice, the better.

[Scene: Breakfast time in a normal house.]

CHARACTERS: Mum
                 Dad
                 Baby
                 Granny

Baby could be small boned teenager or very good younger actor or actress.
[Thoughts heard as voice over]

SCENE 1

[Curtain up as mum puts baby in high chair]

VO:	Oh God, back in this straight jacket again.
MUM:	There we are my little cherabimbimbim, it's brekky wekky time again.
VO:	About bloody time, too.

BABY:	Goo goo goo.
MUM:	Now, let's just put your bibby wibby on.
BABY:	Goo goo ga.
VO:	For God's sake, why don't you speak normally?

[Enter Dad]

DAD:	[To wife] Morning, darling. [Goes to baby and kisses him on the head] Hey champ, how's my little soldier today?
BABY:	Ga ga goo.
VO:	Bloody hungry. Mum is still trying to undo the jar.
DAD:	What's he having this morning?
MUM:	I thought I'd try him on this new organic cereal.
VO:	I bet you haven't tried it first.
BABY:	Ga ga goo.
MUM:	Here you are, my little cherrabimbimbim.
BABY:	Bim bim bim.
MUM:	There's a clever little lovely. [To Dad] Did you hear that, darling? He copied my words.
VO:	You wouldn't like it if I copied the words you use on the phone when Dad's not here.
MUM:	Now cherrabimbimbim, open wide. (Puts spoon in mouth) You'll just love this.
VO:	If it's so bloody good, why don't you eat it?
BABY:	[Coughs and splutters. Spits it out]
MUM:	Ooh darling, come along, it's good for you. [Tries another spoon]
BABY:	[Same reaction]
VO:	No chance – it's not sweet enough.
DAD:	Maybe it's too dry.
MUM:	Well, I followed the instructions on the jar.
BABY:	[Coughs]
VO:	That'll be a first.
MUM:	[Tries] I think I'll add a little sugar.
DAD:	Not too much – it's bad for his teeth.
VO:	I haven't got any yet – pillock.
BABY:	[Starts to cry a little]
	Ba ba eethy.

MUM:	There there, now open wide Tries another spoon]
BABY:	[Takes and swallows]
VO:	That's more like it.
BABY:	Eacky beacky ood.
MUM:	Do you know darling, I think he is trying to talk already. [Gives another spoon]
DAD:	Well, of course. [To baby] You know what you want, don't you champ?
BABY:	Ga ga gamp.
DAD:	Champ – say champ.
BABY:	Camp, camp. [Both parents laugh]
Dad:	No – 'champ champ'.
BABY:	Camp, champ.
DAD:	Do you know, I think you are right.
MUM:	Oh, by the way, your mum rang first thing while you were in the shower. [Still feeding baby]
DAD:	What does the old witch want this time?
BABY:	Itch itch witch. [Not quite clear. Chuckles]
MUM:	She wants to know if we need her for babysitting tonight – you know, we did talk about going over to John and Silvie's.
VO:	Oh no, grandma's not coming, I hope. She smells worse than my nappies.
DAD:	Damn, I had forgotten. Yes, we could go. Are we expected?
MUM:	Well, sort of. It's just kind of arrive, and nibbles and a glass. [Puts in last spoon] There we are, a nice clean bowl. Good boy, Zak.
BABY:	Goo goo cak cak.
VO:	Thank God that's done.
MUM:	Zak – say Zak.
BABY:	Tries to mimic] Cak cak Zak.
DAD:	Hey, that's terrific! – Try saying my name. M i c h a e l.
BABY:	Ical ical mm.
DAD:	Michael.

VO:	I thought your name was John. That's who mum is always on the phone to.
BABY:	Mmmmical bon bon uv uv.
MUM	[Face questioning, slightly concerned]
	What did you say, darling?
BABY:	Uv bon bon.
DAD:	He is certainly coming out with some new sounds.
MUM:	[Slightly on guard]
	Darling, that's wonderful
BABY:	Wun wun bon bon.
MUM:	What are you trying to say, Zak? Try dad dad dad, mum mum mum.
VO:	I can say John.
DAD:	Has he finished his drink? You know that's important.
	[He starts putting papers into case]
MUM:	Yes, I am just giving him the last drops. Here you are darling, finish this up.
BABY:	Dop dop dop, don don don
	[Takes drink and spits it out]
DAD:	Hey champ, say Michael. MY CAL. [Repeats]
BABY:	Mmical mmical. [Chuckles] Bim bim itch itch ww ww ww.
VO:	I must slow down. I'll get into trouble.
DAD:	Zak, that's really clever.
BABY:	[Chuckles] Zak zak zak. [Chuckles]
DAD:	Well, I must dash. I will be late for the meeting.
	[Kisses Zak] Bye champ.
	[Kisses Mum] See you later, darling.

[FADE TO BLACK]

SCENE 2

[Lights come up to evening. They are going out and Granny is arriving shortly.]

MUM:	Arranging baby in high chair]
	There we are my little cherub. Granny will give you your supper. She will be here in a minute.
BABY:	Cherub minute, cherub minute.
VO:	Smelly old bag.
DAD:	[Enters]
	Hi darling, how has your day been?
MUM:	Oh fine, just tiring.
DAD:	How's my little champ?
BABY:	Goo goo [Chuckles]
DAD:	[Enters] What time is the old witch getting here?
BABY:	Old itch, old itch.
VO :	God. I hope she's had a shave. She's got more hair on her chin than the cat.
BABY:	Itch itch itch itch, ha ha ha.
	[Parents seem not to hear as they tidy]
MUM:	I wish you wouldn't call her the old witch. I know she can be trying, but she means well.
BABE:	Well well, witch witch.
MUM:	[Suddenly] Did you hear that, Mike? He's repeating what I said.
VO:	That could be embarrassing, couldn't it, Mummy dear?
BABY:	Sed sed sed.
DAD:	Well, he is a bright boy. He is learning fast
BABY:	Fart fart fart.
	[Both look and laugh]
DAD/MUM:	Fast fast fast.
DAD:	Hey champ, you are a winner. Oh, I hear a car outside, that'll be her.
MUM:	Right, I'll get my coat. Bye bye sweetheart, be good for Granny.

VO:	I hope you've left a clean nappy in the cupboard.
BABY:	Bye bye bye.
	[Doorbell rings]
MUM:	I'll see you in the morning.
DAD:	Bye bye soldier.
	[Voice off as Granny comes in. Enter Granny]
GRANNY:	Hello my lovely.
BABY:	Hello, you old witch.

[BLACK OUT]

VO: Here is a Health and safety warning.

        "Never play leapfrog with a unicorn."

A FEW WORDS

This monologue can be used as a filler between scenes or as a link to some other item.

The actor should be plum in the mouth and condescending to the audience.

Generally exaggerate 'a few words'.

VICAR: Dear friends, I feel I must say just a few words – a few words – but in a few words one can often say enough or [Chuckles] sometimes more than enough. I suppose it really all depends on what one is trying – in a few words – to say and of course the time in which one has to say – a few words.

Dear friends, how many times have you heard in a few words – some profound thought or greeting simply put in just a few words?

Dear friends, simple they may be but were they enough. Indeed have you ever asked yourself the simple question – in a few words – am I getting enough?

Dear friends, even in these few words – are you getting enough – there is a feeling of simple yet profound language. Even here, there may be a sense of extra or spare words and so, my dear friends, you might need to ask yourself if you have actually come across a bit of spare.

[Looks hard at someone in the front row]

Perhaps in a few words I can give another example in a few words.

Dear friends, on occasions it has been my duty to visit establishments of night time entertainment and you know the power of a few words has sometimes very profound goodness and meaning. An example might be 'I love uniforms' and 'do you want a good time?' Dear friends, in these simple words – 'do you want a good time?' and 'I love uniforms'– there is the sound of a very caring human being, expressly concerned for one's welfare and happiness.

'Do you want a good time?' assumes that you are having a bad time and so, in these few simple words, 'a good time' is an implied prospect that a caring human can make another feel better.

Yet again, 'I love uniforms' in a few words exclaims admiration for one's appearance and another's love and desire to be dominated.

So, dear friends, in a few words as I come to the end of my few words I would like to leave this thought with you – in a few words –

As we journey through life, gathering, then discarding baggage along the way, we should keep an iron grip, to the very end, on the capacity for silliness. It preserves one from desiccation.

Remember this:

"Tis better to have loved and lost than live with a psycho the rest of your life"

So Blessed is he who expects nothing, for he shall never be disappointed.

[FADE TO BLACK]

VO: "Beggars may be operating in this hall. Please do NOT encourage these professional beggars.
If you have any spare change, please give it to me.

Now, as we break for the interval, I must remind you that prices at the bar may vary depending upon the attitude of the customer."

AM I ENGLISH – OR WHAT?

Politically Correct Insanity

[Scene: An office of the DSS somewhere.

An applicant is being interviewed regarding his claim.

Official is typical civil service nerd. Totally void of common sense or humanity.

Applicant could be either male or female. Honest, hardworking, contributed all of life, etc. and now seeks help.]

[As curtain opens, Smith sits at desk opposite official]

OFFICIAL: You are?

SMITH: Mr. Smith.

OFFICIAL: Christian names?

SMITH: Richard Ian Peter.

OFFICIAL: [Writing]

Mr. Smith, R.I.P.

SMITH: That's correct.

OFFICIAL: And you are claiming assistance for?

SMITH: Housing.

OFFICIAL: Ah, yes. [Turning paperwork]

So, what do you base your claim for housing benefit on, Mr. Smith?

SMITH: Well, I was born here and worked – paid my taxes and all that till I was ill and lost my job – well, retired actually.

OFFICIAL:	And how old are you?
SMITH:	79. I have worked since I was 16.
OFFICIAL:	And what is your nationality?
SMITH:	[Taken aback] English, of course. What do I look like?
OFFICIAL:	Ah – there lies a problem. You should say European.
SMITH:	But I'm not European, I'm English.
OFFICIAL:	Can you prove it?
SMITH:	[Taken by surprise] Can I prove it? Of course I can bloody prove it. I can trace my family back seven generations at least.
OFFICIAL:	Yes, that may be so, but –
SMITH:	But? What do you mean, but? I was born in the Black Country.
OFFICIAL:	[Draws breath] We don't actually refer to that part of the country by that name. We call it the Grey Country.
SMITH:	[In disbelief] What – what are you talking about?
OFFICIAL:	Simply this – we do not call it the 'Black Country' any more.
SMITH:	Why not? That's what it's called and always has been.
OFFICIAL:	Yes, but things – times – have changed. We now have to choose descriptions more carefully so as not to upset people's feelings.
SMITH:	Choose descriptions, upset people's feelings? You are talking nonsense.
OFFICIAL:	I am talking about not offending people.
SMITH:	Offending people. What people? You are offending me right now. I was born there but it doesn't offend me to hear it called the Black Country. For God's sake, stop talking rubbish.
OFFICIAL:	As I say, Mr. Smith, not offending people.
SMITH:	Are you mad?
OFFICIAL:	Ah! Now that's another thing.
SMITH:	Now what?
OFFICIAL:	You mustn't say mad.
SMITH:	Why not?

OFFICIAL: Because by using the word 'mad' you're implying a potential mental condition and even if the poor unfortunate person had such a condition it should be referred to as one who is mentally challenged – quite apart from the fact that their human rights are not to be insulted.

SMITH: Mentally chall … , Look, sonny, I don't know what planet you're from but you are talking bloody rubbish.

OFFICIAL: Mr. Smith, please calm down.

SMITH: Calm down? Calm down? I come down here to sort out my legal benefits and all you've done so far is confuse me with foreign language.

OFFICIAL: It is simply a question of removing offensive words from our conversation, which is laid down in the European convention.

SMITH: Bollocks.

OFFICIAL: I beg your pardon?

SMITH: You heard!

OFFICIAL: [Prepares to get up] Right, that's enough!

SMITH: Okay, so you're a bit of a nutter – sorry, mentally challenged. Now, what about my bloody housing benefit then? When can I have some money? What about my human rights?

OFFICIAL: [Looks at paperwork] Well now, let me see if you have completed all the forms. [Looks through]

SMITH: Yes, bloody paperwork. 32 pages of questions – took nearly a week.

OFFICIAL: Sorry, you cannot say 'weak'. That implies someone physically disadvantaged.

SMITH: I can't believe I'm hearing this. I'm not talking about *someone,* I'm talking about a time period, you moron.

OFFICIAL: Ah, that may be so, but language like that can easily be misunderstood.

SMITH: By whom? Apart from some politically correct bloody idiot like you who no doubt thinks Brussels is the centre of the universe – bloody Euro prat.

OFFICIAL:	Well, perhaps persons who do not have your grasp of the Eng– the national language.
SMITH:	[Seizing the chance] Mother tongue?
OFFICIAL:	Yes, mother tongue.
SMITH:	And what do you mean, exactly?
OFFICIAL:	Well, the language that is generally spoken in our country.
SMITH:	Which is?
OFFICIAL:	Eng– Oh very clever. You nearly caught me there, didn't you? [Gets up for another file]
SMITH:	[Aside] You ought to be caught because you've obviously escaped from a bloody loony bin.
OFFICIAL:	I am sorry – what did you say?
SMITH:	Nothing that you would understand because it was in plain English. Now what about my claim?
OFFICIAL:	[Looks stern. Decides not to bite. Goes back to the paperwork] Now, I see you haven't answered a couple of questions here.
SMITH:	Oh really? Only a couple out of 120 is not bad for an old 'un. Which ones?
OFFICIAL:	Well, here on page 4, look, this one.
SMITH:	[Takes paper and looks] You must be joking. Can't you work that out for yourself?
OFFICIAL:	We are not allowed to.
SMITH:	What are you not allowed to do – use your common sense?
OFFICIAL:	What do you mean by that exactly?
SMITH:	Well, you know how old I am. My date of birth is on the first page.
OFFICIAL:	Yes, I am aware of that.
SMITH:	Well, would I be looking for a job at my age?
OFFICIAL:	Well, I have known persons of senior years seeking an occupation.
SMITH:	Are you out of your mind? I am almost 80. The only occupation I am looking for is testing the chairs in an old folk's home.
OFFICIAL:	I'll ignore that remark. Now, you have overlooked another – number 27.

SMITH:	Which is?
OFFICIAL:	Are you currently claiming child allowance?
SMITH:	[Beside himself with astonishment and amusement] Child allowance? – at my age! I should be so lucky. On my pension I can't afford Viagra even if I wanted it. You really are out of your tiny civil service mind!
OFFICIAL:	Now then, Mr Smith, you cannot use language that infers a different mental plane.
SMITH:	Well, for God's sake, this is ridiculous. [Stands to go]
OFFICIAL:	Ah now, let's keep a sense of proportion, shall we? It is obviously an oversight.
SMITH:	Why couldn't you just tick the boxes yourself? You know my date of birth.
OFFICIAL:	Ah, but we are not allowed to.
SMITH:	Allowed to? The trouble is you can't think like a normal person. [Stands, takes deep breath and walks around for a moment. Becomes composed]
SMITH:	Right, I have had enough of this, I want to see your manager.
OFFICIAL:	Now Mr. Smith, I don't think that will be necessary. I am sure I can sort this out. Anyway, he is out of the office at the moment.
SMITH:	[Interrupting as anger mounts] Well get on with it then. I have had just about enough of your PC crap.
OFFICIAL:	Now, Mr. Smith.
SMITH:	NOW!
OFFICIAL:	[Getting up] There is no need to shout, Mr. Smith.
SMITH:	[Gets up and paces about] There is every need. You are a disgrace. You are not helping me but treating me like a second class citizen. I intend to write and [Pauses, has a thought] and – and congratulate your manager and this office for finding employment for some unfortunate

substandard folk who are not in control of their common sense.

OFFICIAL: [Outraged] substandard?

SMITH: Yes. In addition, it is obvious that someone like me will get no help but if I were an asylum seeker being accommodated in the hotel on the seafront, you would have five people round there helping me fill in the paperwork which would enable me to receive every benefit available.

OFFICIAL: How dare you speak to me like that?

SMITH: I dare because I am an Englishman in my own country. I've worked hard and paid my taxes all my life, never broken the law, and now I find some bloody idiot like you who doesn't know his arse from his elbow standing between me and my rights.

OFFICIAL: [Stands and gathers up paperwork] I think you'd better leave and make another appointment when you are calmer.

SMITH: I'm not leaving till I've got what I came for.

OFFICIAL: And what was that? Remind me.

SMITH: I don't believe this. I am in my own country – I am white, *English,* and I expect to be treated as such.

OFFICIAL: That, Mr. Smith, is exactly why I am giving you such a hard time.

[BLACK OUT]

VO: Here is a Health and Safety announcement for gentlemen
        – "Please be advised that loose fitting underwear may be
        required when taking certain pills."

SEW

[Scene: Lectern] [Speaker walks on, yawns, looks at audience and yawns again.]

Good evening – well I suppose it is.
It gives me the meanest of pleasure to unwelcome you to this the first seminar of SEW – the Society of Effluential Waffologists.
In my capacity as foundling of SEW, I am deluded and totally underwhelmed by your attendance here tonight.

At this inaugural evening I cannot say that we welcome those of you who may be eligible for membership.

[Yawns again]

The current membership does tend to vary, but it is certain that at present the number of fully paid up Waffologists is two.
Apart from, of course, more than six hundred in the House of Commons.

I have already – my life – discounted the number journalists and Z-list celebs who have applied for membership.
I am, however, unsurprised by the number of applications we have received from the how much money can I make – sorry – legal profession.

Remember, these are the people who on the one hand make a fortune out of you slipping on a banana skin when you are too stupid to look where you are going, and on the other by prolonging the court cases of those whom the Home Office have already decided to deport, thus making even more money.

I would also like to welcome representatives of the local synod here this evening .I am aware there was the threat of a boycott – a veiled threat, anyway...

Synod – now there is an interesting if odd word. Sorry, no pun intended. I would suggest that to sin is not odd at all but a perfectly normal reaction to some situations.
In fact, if you turn the word around you do get the oddsin.

But to sin is thought to be evil. So apparently said a man who arguably was the first gay in the village. Well gentlemen, would you spend many many days wandering in the desert with twelve other chaps for fun?

Those who pontificate on such things are indeed masters of Waffology and claim to create something out of nothing – for example, wine from water at the wave of a hand. If only!
Mind you when you listen to so called expert wine tasters you might think they are masters of Waffology.
I heard one only the other day who said:
"This is a great red from the sunny region on the southern slopes of Afghanistan. You can smell the waste from the local tribesman which is sprayed on to the vines just before harvest. This, of course, is neutralised by the influence of the cocaine produced in the adjacent fields.
You then have the unique taste of crap cocaine. More commonly known crack cocaine over here. So this wine known as Taliban Shiraz is distinctive, if nothing else."
So, now for the main topic of my talk.

> "To drink, or not to drink,
> that is the question.
> To imbibe in quantity
> or sup pure quality.
> To dine with fine wine
> which indeed is divine"

So – to drink or not to drink.

Actually, why is it a question? I have it on good authority that none of you are teetotal but as we get older our tastes change, and not always through desire, but more likely a need to minimise the number of times we rush to the toilet.

Remember when we were young and could probably drink copious amounts of beer? Ah, those were the days. But even then, when we drank only three pints, it often felt as though we were getting rid of six.

But slowly, as the years have passed, we may well have turned to and developed a taste for wine.
After all, with wine there is much less demand on our personal plumbing systems. And in that department, maybe there lies a problem for some of us.

Yes, I hear you say, and see you nod in agreement.
In later life, visits to the loo become more of an inconvenience – if you will pardon the pun – for a variety of reasons. So, one wine producer has come up with a possible answer.

A wine co-operative in California has created something unique which helps us remain comfortable a lot longer.
Following medical research they have developed a hybrid of a very well-known and much loved wine variety.

I am talking about a grape type we are all familiar with. The current range of these wines includes Pinot Rouge, Pinot Noir, Pinot Rose and of course Pinot Grigio.

Now, I suggest indeed strongly recommend you try the wine created from this new grape variety and I can assure you that eventually you will feel the benefits, so please raise a glass to this new wine from a Californian vineyard and Pinot More.

Gosh, is that the time? I must just tell you this story before I go.
I was in a plane crossing London when the pilot came on the tannoy and said:
"We are just about to fly over the houses of Parliament, so if you are in the toilet please flush it now".

Thank you and good night.

[BLACKOUT]

VO: "Please be advised that senior citizens should be warned against eating too much healthy food. Surely at a certain age it becomes necessary to take more preservatives."

GRAB IT AND RUN

[Scene: Office of Compensation Solicitors
                   Solicitor Jason sits at desk.]

[Buzz from door. Smith picks up handset.]

Jason: Grab it and Run Solicitors, can I help you?
                   [Pause]
                   Oh hello, Mr Smith, please come up. We are on
                   the second floor.

[Enter he – Bandage round head and limping]

Jason: Good morning, Mr. Smith.
Smith: Morning. Thanks for seeing me.
Jason: Please take a seat. So – what can I do for you?
                   How can I help?
Smith: Well, as you can see, I have had a bit of an
                   accident and I saw your advert for no win no fee
                   claims.
Jason: That's us, Grab and Run compensation lawyers
                   at your service – at a cost, of course.
Smith: At a cost? But no win, no fee.
Jason: Ah yes, but if we win – and we usually do – we
                   do cover our costs.
Smith: Oh, okay – well, that's fair, I suppose. So, how
                   does it work exactly?
Jason: Well, I need to get all the details, Where it
                   happened, injury or damage, date, time of day –
                   witnesses – copy of accident book entry, any
                   medical assistance you had. Once that is written

	up I submit a case and claim from the other party in question.
Smith:	If I win, how much am I likely to get?
Jason:	That, of course, depends on the circumstances and resulting injury, but usually I am looking at making a minimum claim for £10k. In some cases it may be a lot higher.
Smith:	As much as that? Wow.
Jason:	Well, of course, from that we take our fee.
Smith:	Oh, so how much will that be?
Jason:	Generally 45%.
Smith:	45%? That's a hell of a lot.
Jason:	On the face of it, but there is a lot of work to do and you will walk away with £5,500 for what looks like just a bump on your head.
Smith:	So a bruise is worth making a claim for?
Jason:	Yes, absolutely.
Smith:	Right.
Jason:	So tell me what happened.
	[He makes notes]
Smith:	Well, it was like this. I was walking down the road, well on the pavement of course.
Jason:	Walking or running?
Smith:	Yes, walking.
Jason:	Why?
Smith:	Well, I was going somewhere.
Jason:	Where?
Smith:	Does it matter?
Jason:	Well it might, but go on.
Smith:	Anyway, I was walking along and–
Jason:	And what?
Smith:	Well, I banged my head.
Jason:	You banged your head.
Smith:	Yes, that's what I said.
Jason:	On what?
Smith:	On a lamppost.
Jason:	On a lamppost. You banged your head on a lamppost.
Smith:	Yes, that is what I said.
Jason:	What were you doing at the time?

Smith:	I was walking down the road.
Jason:	But were you looking at anything or talking to anyone at the time?
Smith:	No, I was on my own. Oh, I was texting my mate.
Jason:	So you were walking along texting?
Smith:	Yes. I do it all the time.
Jason:	So you were looking down at your phone texting?
Smith:	Yes, I suppose I was.
Jason	So you were not looking where you were going?
Smith:	No, I suppose I wasn't.
Jason:	And as a result you walked straight into a lamppost?
Smith:	Well, yes.
Jason:	Did you see any signs warning you that lampposts might cause an obstruction?
Smith:	No, of course not. Why should there be signs for lampposts?
Jason:	They are an obstruction, and thereby might pose a hazard to passersby.
Smith:	Well, what about things like rubbish bins or pillar boxes?
Jason:	Well, the same rules should apply.
Smith:	So, hang on a minute – are you saying that any obstruction to pedestrians should have a warning triangle in front of it?
Jason:	Yes, of course. People have a right to be warned of something that may cause them to have an accident.
Smith:	Does that apply anywhere?
Jason:	Pretty much, yes. That's why I am here to help you make a successful claim.
Smith:	Great, thanks. Just another query – you said earlier that a bruise is worth making a claim for?
Jason:	Yes, I did – yes it is.
Smith:	So do the same rules apply inside a building as well as in the street?
Jason:	Well, of course. Why do you ask?

Smith: Because when I came in your front door I hurt my leg on the filing cabinet in the hall. There were no warning triangles, so I am going to sue you for damages.

[BLACKOUT]

SHOPPING

[Speaker either male or female]

Good evening and welcome to the Society of Shopaholics and another in a series of talks on modern behaviour in the high street.

Tonight's talk is entitled, "How to rule the roost when shopping in your local supermarket."

We all use these stores, but it is important to understand and follow certain rules and practices when shopping to establish your authority.

So, let's take it step by step.

First, for those of you who drive to the store car park, there are some basic rules to follow.

1   Never park in a designated bay. If two bays are empty make sure you straddle the central white line completely.

      However if that's not possible park beyond the end of the row in a non-designated area.

      This will annoy and create angry and frustrated drivers looking for a parking spot.

      It also ensures that shoppers with trolleys are forced away from walking routes.

2   Having left your car, ensure you walk slowly down the centre of the main driveway thereby further slowing down other incoming customers.

      If you have young children with you, make sure they run all over the place causing more raised tempers and annoyance to incoming drivers.

3   Now it's time to collect your trolley.
Always ensure you pick one which you cannot control owing to the fact that the wheels steer themselves in the opposite direction to the one you want.
This will ensure your trolley continuously bumps into other shoppers or their trolleys.

4   Now, when you go into the store remember to enter via the designated exit. This causes delays to those on their way out. It may also set off an alarm which will wake up the security person at the desk.

5   Right, now for the shopping. Get your shopping list out and start looking for the items. You soon realise that cheese is not on the shelf next to shampoo. So you need to turn the trolley crossways in the aisle while you look at the signs hanging from the ceiling, thus causing obstruction to others and staff filling the shelves.

6   After many minutes and with several items now in the trolley, you see a friend and stop to have a chat. Remember to park your trolley next to them and not in line. This will ensure you block more of the aisle and annoy other shoppers.

7   There will be a point when your mobile phone rings. So that everyone in the store can hear you, make sure you speak in a very loud voice especially when you say things like, "No they don't sell them here, I will have to go to a chemist".
When you finish your call, always make sure you say 'Bye bye' at least 10 times as your voice rises to a shriek.

8   Of course, very young children these days apparently are meant to be heard more than seen.
Hear them you certainly can – so if yours are shouting and/or screaming, just ignore them and you will find other shoppers suddenly give you more space.
If your children are a bit older, let them run round the store – after all, they probably need the exercise. In the

process they may bump into someone who has just taken a glass jar of something from a shelf.

This will result in the following in store tannoy announcement,

VO: "Will the store cleaner please go to aisle 5, where some uncontrolled little brat has caused an accident."

Or words to that effect.

9   So, finally you get to the check out. When half of your items have been swiped at the till, you suddenly realise you have forgotten something which happens to be at the other end of the store. Never mind that there are six people already queuing behind you. You wander off to get said item returning several minutes later to hear the cashier apologising yet again

10   At last all your items are through the checkout and into bags in the trolley. Now it is time to pay. But where is your wallet or purse? You suddenly remember it is in a bag, but which one? You begin to search, then remember it is in your jacket pocket, but never mind, you have delayed the others for a few more minutes.

11   Eventually you make your way back to your car and put your shopping in the boot. Now you have to get rid of your trolley, but do not take it to a trolley bay if there is an empty car space nearby. Dump it there and you will cause more frustration to customer when they come in.

So there you have it. A few simple rules to   follow when going to your supermarket. Of course, if you would prefer to be in the minority, do not follow any of these rules.

Thank you for listening.

[BLACK OUT]

OPENING AN ACCOUNT

[Scene: Bank/Building Society Desk, 2 chairs, Official at desk]

[Enter client]

Banker:	Please take a seat Mr. Er…
Bond:	Bond – thank you.
Banker:	Now, Mr Bond, I see you have applied to open a savings account with us.
Bond:	Yes, that's right. I need to transfer some bonds.
Banker:	Are they your wife's bonds, Mr Bond?
Bond:	No, my own bonds.
Banker:	So one bond – in the name of Bond into our bonds.
Bond:	Yes, that's right.
Banker:	Right, well I just need to go through your application form to clarify a few details.
Bond:	Okay, what do you need to know?
Banker:	Your name is Bond, Jamie Bond?
Bond:	Yes.
Banker:	And your father's name?
Bond:	Well, Bond of course.
Banker:	And what was your mother's maiden name?
Bond:	Bond.
Banker:	No, I mean her maiden name.
Bond:	Bond.
Banker:	Sorry, I am getting confused – your father's name is Bond?
Bond:	Yes.
Banker:	And your mother's maiden name was Bond?

Bond:	Yes.
Banker:	Isn't that rather odd?
Bond:	We were a very close community.
Banker:	I see. Yes, well, let's move on. Now you give your address as: Mail Box 16, Spooks Mansion, Vauxhall Bridge.
Bond:	Yes, that is correct.
Banker:	I mention it because you have written 'box number'. Should that be apartment number?
Bond:	No, all my post goes to M16.
Banker:	And how long have you been there?
Bond:	About 6 months.
Banker:	And your previous address was?
Bond:	I was in Berlin.
Banker:	And how long where you there?
Bond:	Again 6 months.
Banker:	Only 6 months? Isn't that rather unusual?
Bond:	Not in my business. Look, can we get on please? I have an appointment in Whitehall.
Banker:	Whitehall – I see [Going down the form] Okay Sir, I need to know your income.
Bond:	Why do you need to know that? I am not asking for a loan.
Banker:	It's just a routine question on all our Kings Growth Bond forms. We are an exclusive bank and only accept special clients.
Bond:	[Smiles] Well, let's say six figures. Did you say Kings Growth Bond?
Banker:	Yes. that's right. Is there a problem?
Bond:	No, I just did not expect to put money into the KGB.
Banker:	KGB. [Laughs] Oh yes, I see what you mean. Goes down the form] Oh yes. Nationality?
Bond:	English.
Banker:	And your employer?
Bond:	Her Majesty's Government.
Banker:	Fine. Now occupation.
Bond:	Why do you need that?
Banker:	It is part of our information requirements.

Bond:	Why? What does it matter where my money comes from – providing it is legal?
Banker:	I am sorry, but I have to complete this form. So, occupation?
Bond:	Assassin.
Banker:	[Hesitates, then smiles] Assassin?
Bond:	Yes.
Banker:	Okay, so who do you assassinate?
Bond:	People who ask too many bloody stupid questions.

[BLACK OUT]

VO: And now we break for a party political broadcast.

PARTY POLITICAL BROADCAST

[Character: male, smartly dressed addressing a public meeting.]

Good afternoon. I warmly welcome all of you to my election talk. For those of you who are first time voters – which I gather includes about 60% of the population – I am here representing the Celebrities and Rubbish Appreciation Party. So, we are commonly known as the CRAP party.

I would like to outline some of our proposals.
First:

EQUALITY
We believe in equality. Therefore, it will become law that everyone dresses in clothes of the opposite sex on Saturdays, thus ensuring we all appreciate each other's comfort zones. Not only will this be quite spectacular, especially at football and rugby matches, but it will also boost the economy of the clothing retail trade.

PUBLIC TRANSPORT
We want to make public transport more friendly, so it will also become law that when boarding a train or bus you will be expected to say hello and shake hands with everyone else in the carriage. This could be particularly interesting on Saturdays when people are dressed in clothing of the opposite sex.

NOW SOMETHING ABOUT IQ LEVELS
Bearing in mind the name of our party, we will require all so-called celebs to take an IQ test. Remember, celebs are to real

talent what McDonald's are to real food. Those who score below 25 – which we suspect will be the majority – will be cast in a new TV series entitled 'They are Celebrities – Leave them There'. We are expecting a large cast.

AIR QUALITY

Pollution is of great concern to us all. Therefore, in the interest of Health and Safety, all citizens will be required to give prior notice to anyone within 20 feet when they are about to pass wind.

ECONOMY AND FOREIGN POLICY

On Foreign policy, we actually mean Home Policy. Our plan is to make each county an independent state.

Thus, the national debt will be reduced so greedy bankers' bonuses will be cut to the bone.

This will involve setting up border controls across the country. We will then set up a neutral banking state – rather like Switzerland. Then, as your government, we can apply for foreign aid from the IMF and EU and give to each county. No doubt each area will have a leader who will then open a Bank Account in our neutral state to stash away any aid that is given. No change there then.

HUMAN RIGHTS

On the issue of so called human rights, we will bring in a policy that gives everyone the right to push custard pies into the faces of journalists who probe into the lives of boring people such as so-called celebrities and politicians. This will not only increase custard pie making, but will also give extra trade to dry cleaners and those greedy lawyers. But hang on, don't they make enough already?

LAW, ORDER AND AGRICULTURE

We propose to bring back the stocks for those who cause local trouble. We will link this idea to the local farming community who will be given backing to increase the tomato crop.

These will then be able to be purchased at a special price for the public to throw at those in the stocks.

So those are some of our key objectives which we strongly believe will improve society.

Therefore, at the next election, please make sure that the party that gets your vote is CRAP. No change there, then.

Thank you and good night.

[BLACKOUT]

WHAT STAG NIGHT?

So, how old is too old for a stag party?

[Scene: 3 old friends meet and wait for the arrival of an 85-year-old friend who is getting married again.]

Nigel:	[Raises his glass] Well, cheers.
Derek:	Cheers. Mm, that tastes good. Well, Martin should be here in a minute unless he has forgotten where we are.
Nigel:	Well, he is getting on a bit so memory does play tricks. He is coming up to 85.
Bill:	Is that right? I must admit I had forgotten that – well, I must say he seems good for his age.
Nigel:	Yes, but what is the point of getting married again at his age?
Derek:	Yes, well I'm not so sure about that either. How long since you have seen him Bill?
Bill:	Several months, I suppose. Why, what's happened?
Derek:	Nothing really, but he is getting a bit rough round the edges – you know, getting things mixed up as we all do.
Nigel:	Yes, his memory is certainly playing tricks. You should have heard him last week.
Bill:	Last week? What happened?
Derek:	Well, it was like this. [Laughs] We went to an Italian bistro for lunch – they had a special offer on and Nigel suggested we give it a go.

Nigel :	[Laughs] Oh yes – that was a laugh. Go on, Derek, tell Bill what happened.
Derek:	Well, we settled in and looked at the menu, then the waiter came over for the order.
Nigel:	Right – yes, that was it.
Derek:	Anyway, Martin decided to have pasta, so he says to the waiter, "I would like some really spicy *spermicelli".*
Nigel:	You should have seen faces turn to look at him – spermicelli indeed! [Laughs again]
Derek:	Anyway, the waiter said calmly [Italian accent] "I think you mean vermicelli – is thicker than spaghetti and it mean "little worms".
Nigel:	Oh yes, so then Martin says, "I don't like worms to eat, I'll have Rigoletto instead".
Bill:	Isn't Rigoletto an opera or some such?
Nigel:	Yes, exactly. Anyway, the waiter said he had never heard pasta sing, so would order rigatoni instead. So, you see, he is beginning to lose it.
Derek:	It was really funny but – oh here he is. [Enter Martin]
Martin:	Hello all – sorry I am a bit late. I couldn't find my teeth.
Bill:	Where were they?
Martin:	What? Sorry, my ear piece is playing up again. [Fiddles with it]
Nigel/Derek:	[All together laugh] So, where were they?
Martin:	Where were what?
Bill:	Your teeth.
Martin:	Oh, in the car.
Derek:	Why did you take them out in the car?
Martin:	Well, erm… Oh, I can't remember. Something to do with chewing gum – it pulled them out.
Bill:	Anyway Martin, what would you like to drink?
Martin:	I'll try a glass of that new one, Pino More.
Nigel:	Right, that'll be the day. When you get to our age, there is often a plumbing problem.
Derek:	That's not fair – you leak for yourself.
Bill:	Ha ha ha. Anyway Martin, why are you getting spliced again? She's not expecting, is she?

Martin:	No she's not expected until later on – she is with her daughter today.
	[They all laugh]
Bill :	No – expecting. Oh, never mind. Now, about your stag weekend – any ideas?
Martin:	Stag weekend – at my age? I don't think I'll be going on one.
Nigel:	Oh yes you are. We are going to organise one for us four, but we need some ideas.
Derek:	How about a powered Zimmer frame race?
	[All laugh]
Martin:	What did you say?
	[He fiddles with hearing aid]
Bill:	A race on a powered Zimmer.
Derek:	I was joking. Is there such a thing?
Bill:	I don't know, but we could easily fit a battery power unit to one and stick some wheels under it.
Nigel:	What about a karaoke night at The Old Bull?
Martin:	[Fiddles again with ear piece] Harry Oakly – I haven't seen him for ages.
Derek:	No Martin – karaoke.
Martin:	What?
Bill:	It is a singing night?
Martin:	Oh – well, I used to sing in a choir. Is it like that?
Nigel:	Well, not exactly, no.
Martin:	What show is it, then?
Bill:	It is an open mic night.
Martin:	Oh, is Mike going to be there?
Derek:	No he isn't. You sing a solo on a mic.
Nigel:	In the local pub. Or we could go pole dancing.
Bill:	Pole dancing – now, there's an idea.
Nigel:	I saw this piece in the paper. They are starting a club near Chelmsford for over eighties to learn pole dancing.
Derek:	Are you serious?
Nigel:	Yes. I've still got the press cutting.
Martin:	What's pole dancing?
Bill:	It's like dancing round a fireman's pole.

Nigel:	Anyway – any other ideas?
Bill:	How about a trip to Clacton to the pier? We could do some bungee jumping.
Derek:	Yes, that sounds good. So long as there is a paramedic on hand.
Martin:	I don't think I could do bungee jumping.
Bill:	Why not?
Martin:	Well, think of where the straps of the harness go.
Derek:	Oh yes, I forgot, you have a bag thing, don't you?
Nigel:	Bag – what bag?
Derek:	You know – the bag that stops you getting caught short.
Martin:	Anyway, what about the fireman's pole you mentioned?
Bill:	You mean pole dancing?
Martin:	Polish dancing?
Derek:	No, Martin – dancing round a pole.
Martin:	Do they mind?
Nigel:	Martin – no they don't. It's like you are dancing with a lamppost.
Martin:	And why would I want to do that? It seems ridiculous.
Nigel:	Right, we need some other ideas. How about a cocktail making session?
Bill:	Actually, that could be a great idea. I know a Hotel in Brighton where they do sessions. We could go down for the weekend. Martin likes a drink.
Martin:	Oh, I like a gin and tonic occasionally and I just about know how to make it.
Derek:	Yes but there is a lot more to cocktails than gin and tonic.
Nigel:	I've actually got some leaflets here for that. [Takes them out of pocket] There are some really funny names of cocktails on the list. In fact, I went in for a competition to write a verse using cocktail names.
Bill:	That sounds interesting.

	[Starts scribbling on a piece of paper] Was it like "Gin sling in the bin"?

Martin: [Starts scribbling on a piece of paper] Was it like "Gin sling in the bin"?

Martin: How about "Vodka and tonic makes you vomit"?

Derek: Oh Martin, please.

Martin: Sorry, only joking.

Nigel: Tell you what – let's look through the brochure and make one up now.

Bill: Yes, good idea.

Derek: Let's have a look.
[Takes paper laughs at some names]
Some of these names are crazy.

Martin: [Looking over his shoulder] Or ridiculous. Look at those; 'Blowtorch' and 'Broken Leg'.

Bill: What about that one then? Pink Pussy.

Nigel: What? [Laughs] What's in it?

Bill: Campari, peach Brandy and bitter lemon. Oh, here is another one – Rusty Nail.

Derek: So, let's see – you could use a Blowtorch on a Rusty Nail, get drunk and have a Broken Leg.

Martin: That would not be the answer to a Maidens Prayer, would it?

Nigel: Yes, and end up in Boot Hill – look, brandy, Bourbon and lemon juice.

Martin: Oh look. some non-alcoholic ones. You could have a Rum Dance with a Wild Dog.

Bill: Right, I think I've got it. Listen to this – "Harvey Wallbanger awoke to a beautiful Tequila Sunrise. He reached out to fondle Margarita Between the Sheets and cut his hand on a Rusty Nail. Bloody Mary, he shouted. Let's go and have Sex on the Beach. Before they could a Volcano erupted. The Scorpion who had been sitting on the rocks was eating a Cool Banana."
[They all laugh]

Derek: That's great. I've heard of some of those. Are they all cocktails?

Bill: Yes, definitely.

Nigel:	Right Bill, that's it. A cocktail weekend in Brighton. Martin, are you happy with that?
Martin:	Yes, that sounds fine. I know the first one I am going to have.
Derek:	What's that?
Martin:	It's Vermouth, Calvados and Brandy.
Bill:	Wow, that sounds good. What is it called?
Martin	What every 85 year old needs before he gets married. A Corpse Reviver.
	[They all laugh and repeat]
	Corpse Reviver.

[FADE TO BLACK]